Dusty
the Church Dog

and other sightings of the gospel

Thom M. Shuman

ISBN: 1490970835
ISBN-13: 978-1490970837

DEDICATION

For Dusty,
now riding shotgun
in God's pick-up truck,
with his head out the window,
hollering,
'go faster, Dad, go faster!'

I wonder what was in the mind of Jesus as he went around calling people to follow.

Was he hoping that folks would follow him as dogs do humans? Trustingly, unconditionally, always hoping for a treat to be pulled out of the pocket and tossed up in the air? All I have to do is get up and out of my chair, and Cocoa the Wonder Dog becomes my inseparable shadow. And if I go anywhere near my shoes, she is ready to follow me to the ends of the earth (as long as we stop for breaks to chase squirrels!).

If that is the sort of response Jesus was hoping for, he was sadly disappointed. For human beings are more like cats than dogs. Finicky, fussy, always wanting to be waited upon, always wanting to have our own way, always believing that others should be able to read our minds and meet our unspoken, yet very definite, expectations.

As much as Peter could proclaim to Jesus, as Cocoa does to us, that he would follow him anywhere, the first time there is a bump in the road, Peter becomes like Paisley the not-so-wonderful cat: willful, spiteful, digging in his claws and refusing to be budged. All so catlike, all so human.

Jesus would have been better off in the first place, just going around and whistling for the dogs to follow him. It would have been a lot easier, a lot simpler.

But he chooses to call us . . . and chooses to be stuck with us as his disciples, trusting and believing that he can transform us from cats into dogs and then into disciples.

walking

One of the fellows in the church claims he saw me out jogging the other day. 'Don't worry,' I told him, 'if you ever see me running, either I am chasing the dog, or Bonnie is after me!' I don't run.

But I love to walk. For years, I would try to walk every day of the week, usually with a tape player 'reading' me a book while I walked. I figured it was a good way to judge my time, since most audio tapes are in the range of 30-45 minutes to a side. And I wouldn't get distracted from my 'mission' to exercise.

But since we got Cocoa the Wonder Dog, my routine has changed. She and I still walk 30-45 minutes a day, but she would not begin to tolerate my wearing headphones and listening to a book. After all, if I did I would miss

- her excitement at seeing a squirrel (don't laugh; when was the last time you got excited over a little creature like that?);

- her intrepid stalking of the cat hiding in the bushes;

- the pure delight in the eyes of every child when they stop and get to pet her;

- the sun peeking over the edge of the world, the moon whispering 'good night', the mist hovering over the lawns, the morning chorale by the birds that beats anything Handel ever wrote.

And now, when I am walking home at lunch, and could put on the tapes to listen to a book, I don't - after all, I might miss one of the delights God has placed along the path.

I don't know if I am burning more calories walking Cocoa;
I doubt if my cardio rate is where it should be . . .

. . . but my soul?

Ah, that is getting a good work-out each and every day!

messy ministry

the 3-volume commentary on Isaiah
gathers dust on the corner of the desk;
the voice-mail bristles with folks
who are not too happy with the
kind of music the youth group
played in worship the other day;

the 'round file' overflows with
the latest reminders
from the judicatory
that the monthly statistics on
pastoral calls, baptisms,
and new members
have not reached the office;

shelves groan with books bought
with good intentions;
sermon manuscripts,
unfinished liturgies,
prayers written on
the backs of bills
litter the floor
around the rocking chair;

just then,
the door bursts open
and a knot of children
from the neighborhood
come crowding in,
laughing and shouting:
"come on,
you promised to tell us a story!"

Smiling a 'thank you'
to the sky,
Jesus gets up
and follows.

Every morning, and most evenings, Cocoa the Wonder Dog rushes out the door, confident that *this* is the moment when she finally catches a squirrel. She is a faithful and diligent searcher, knowing every tree that her adversaries have ever climbed to escape (why else would we stop at every single one we pass?). She knows that if she was only a little more sneaky, a little quicker, those pesky gray critters could not elude her again.

Of course, the reality is that if she ever caught a squirrel she would be so surprised that she wouldn't know what to do with it. One time, we were passing a tree in which a squirrel was noisily giving Cocoa the 'razzberry' when it suddenly fell out of the tree and landed a foot from Cocoa's nose. I'm not sure who was more shocked, but the squirrel came to its senses quicker than Cocoa did, and once again, the quarry eluded the Wonder Dog.

Every morning, and most evenings (and all the moments in between), I rush out the door, confident that *this* will be the day I finally catch God. I know where God is (why else would I keep visiting every place I have ever seen God?). I know what I want from God. And if I am just a little more prayerful, just a little more humble, just a little more pious, God can't elude me too much longer.

Then I stop, and look down, and realize that it is God who has been chasing me, God who has been searching everywhere for me, God who has finally 'treed' me . . .
. . .just waiting for me to fall out of my nice, safe, comfortable life, where I have gone to escape, so I can be caught in the arms of everlasting love, joy, hope, and peace.

I used to look forward to summer. It was that time when things slowed down, when folks could take a deep breath and relax, when I had time to catch up on reading all the books and journals that had accumulated during the program year of the church.

But not anymore.

Since the beginning of the 21st century, it seems that the summer months have been just as harried, just as frazzled, just as maniacal as the other nine months. There is no real let up in demands, in needs, in meetings, in expectations. And it's not just true for churches and for pastors, I hear a lot of folks describing summer as a season of stress, not sand, sunshine, and sipping tea. It reflects our cult of busyness.

We are too busy to sit out on the deck and listen to a ballgame on the radio. And if we do, we have our laptop or tablet at our fingertips, multi-tasking.

We're too busy to have neighbors over for a cook-out, or even a simple dessert.

We're too busy to keep in touch with those friends and family members who can help us connect with the core of who we are.

We're even too busy for God, who blesses us with crystal clear nights filled with stars, summer mornings of stunning sunrises, crickets willing to lull us to sleep as dusk slowly falls.

Busyness keeps us from falling silent enough to listen to God whisper in our ears; busyness keeps us from putting down our stress and picking up a glove to play toss with our daughter; busyness has us always running on the treadmill of success rather than walking hand-in-hand with our partner; busyness fills our hearts and souls with bitterness and regret.

Jesus was once accused of being an accomplice of Beelzebul ('lord of the house'). The demon we pal around with all summer should be called Beelzebusy - lord of the overload.

hopscotch

As Cocoa the Wonder Dog was taking me on my morning walk, we once again came across that ancient hieroglyphic known as "Hopscotch." Drawn in chalk by one of the little people in the neighborhood, it offered a tantalizing invitation to turn back the clock. Yesterday, I was able to resist; today, I just had to give in to the urge.

And so, while Cocoa covered her eyes with her paw in great embarrassment, I played the game once more. Of course, my adult-sized feet had trouble fitting in the child size squares, and my dexterity is not what it was when I was six or seven, but I made it!

What joy, what fun, what memories came flooding back! And how delighted I am that in this age of video games, internet, email, and text messaging, there are still children who grab a piece of chalk, mark out the lines, and play a game that is older than I am.

It's those simple games, those memories from earlier years, those comforts we carry around stored inside of us just waiting to be opened at the right moment, which can encourage us, strengthen us, support us in times of great despair and pain.

It's like when I lay in bed after a long day filled with disappointment, struggles, and questions about God's presence in my life. I can't begin to pray . . . until I reach back to those childhood nights of long ago, and pray once again: 'now I lay me down to sleep,
          I pray the Lord my soul to keep;
          if I should die before I wake,
          I pray the Lord my soul to take.'

And the next thing I know, I wake up, rested from being held in the arms of the One who never sleeps.

For most of us, our first experience of death is that of a pet, when we are children.

A little girl in the church lost her pet cat the other day. It got into the street and was run over by a car. Of course, the little girl was devastated and her mother had the usual difficulty of trying to explain what had happened, and what death means.

Down the street lived a neighbor. Less educated than most, economically challenged, a descendent of folks from Appalachia (where the "hillbillies" live in America). A woman that most of us would overlook if we passed her on the street.

But that evening, while Talea was crying herself to sleep, this neighbor gathered up hot water, rags, and cleaning supplies, and went out into the street, and scrubbed clean the spot where the kitten had died A random act of kindness so that Talea would not have to be reminded of what had happened to her beloved pet whenever she walked down the street.

The best Samaritans are always the ones we least expect.

The dog days of faith are here.

The Middle East continues to be a powder keg just waiting to explode; the terror alerts come and go so often we can't remember how we are supposed to feel; folks continue to exhibit boorish behavior towards those who look, dress, talk differently from them, a trait we had hoped had finally disappeared from the world.

And a person of faith wonders what can one person do to bring peace, reconciliation, hope to such brokenness?

The city in which I live can't seem to find enough money to keep swimming pools open (much less repair them to any sort of decent shape) in the summer for the neediest of our families, but the leaders want to increase the local sales tax to build a new, bigger jail.

And a person of faith wonders how do you convince people that their priorities might be wrong?

In a few short weeks, school will be starting. Some of our children will head off to school without the school supplies they need (because they can't afford them); kids will go to school hungry (because parents have to choose between medicine or food); kids will go to school without the 'right' clothes (because some can't even afford the uniforms that are supposed to save families money). And they will walk into schools that are crumbling physically, falling down emotionally, and have become easy targets because 'the schools don't teach our kids "values!" '

And a person of faith wonders if anyone sees the value in providing the tools all of the children in our communities need to survive in life, much less succeed.

The dog days of faith are here.

And we can only pray that a cool front of compassion will sweep in and break the oppressive hate wave which dominates our world. We can only pray that living water will pour down and end the drought of despair which has gripped us. We can only pray that the lethargy of hopelessness which has sapped our energy will be gone in the morning after a good night's rest in the heart of the One who never sleeps.

The dog days of faith are here . . .

can we get through them?

It's a new day in heaven, and once again, music will be played.

Jesus is at the piano, plinking a lonely melody for all the kids who have struggled for life, and with life, since they were born; for the crack/heroin babies, those whose birth mothers drank during pregnancy, special needs; all those who never got the second chance at a home, a family, a love they deserved; for all those teenage girls and boys who come home from school to find the locks have been changed and a suitcase has been left on the front porch with all that the family thinks they deserve.

Lazarus is gently playing his snare drum with his brushes, retelling the images of people still trying to rebuild their lives, their homes, their communities after hurricanes, tsunamis, earthquakes.

Mary Magdalene is loosening up her voice, cradling in her heart the laments from the mothers of Lebanon, Israel, Iraq, New Orleans, Afghanistan, the West Bank, and all the other shattered communities in the world.

God is dragging his scarred and battered bass out, ready to play a beat which will reverberate in the people who profess umbrage at innocent children who are abused and killed, yet are not outraged by the politicians who cut services to our children; by people who talk as if homeland security is more crucial than secure, safe, and affordable homes for our neighbors; by people who pray for peace, but cannot seem to make it a reality in our lives.

Some of the tunes are those that have been played since creation first burst forth into the world, and some are just little ditties that have been running around and around the universe, just waiting for someone to grab hold of them and share them with everybody who is willing to listen.

It's a new day in heaven, and once again, the blues will be played.

No more wet sloppy kisses in the morning; no more keeping my back warm during the night.

No more miserable walks in bone-chilling rain; no more bounding through the snow on a winter's evening.

No more protecting her 'castle' from the daily onslaught by the postal service; no more barking at the invisible dogs parading down her sidewalk. No more squirrel-chasing, cat-aggravating, bouncing-like-Tigger-for-treats adventures; no more lazing in the sunshine on the back deck.

No more trying to fit in my lap because that is what the cat is able to do; no more loud snores on the sofa as we try to watch TV. No more unbridled excitement whenever we touch our shoes or jackets; no more "I missed you terribly" crying when I walk in the door.

No more looks with eyes that melt the most hardened heart; no more unconditional love that makes every miserable moment of any miserable day disappear.

No more.

Cocoa the Wonder Dog died last night.

It was as unexpected as the Spirit coming down on that first day of Pentecost, and it leaves a hole the size of Hurricane Katrina in my heart.

In the book "All Dogs Go to Heaven," the author talks about heaven overflowing with squirrels, and the dogs all sleeping with God (if that's so, watch out, God; Cocoa likes her space!).

Now, I am commanded to love God with all my Reformed, modern, well-educated mind, which tells me that this is a nice way to try to comfort kids on the death of a beloved pet. Really???

But . . .

. . . since I am also commanded to love God with all my heart, I will hope for that day to come when Cocoa will come bounding up to me, tail wagging, eyes dancing, ready to go on that walk which will never have to end.

Whenever some tells me that the Bible is an old, dusty, archaic, should-remain-on-the-shelf-unopened book that has absolutely no relevance for today, I take one and open it to Hebrews 11, hand it to them, and say, "Read this."

It's all the stories of the Bible in one chapter; it's the theology of the Bible that can be read in just a couple of minutes; it's the reminder that despite all our best efforts, all our brilliance, all our human achievements, it all boils down to one thing: faith.

Faith is what inspires us, faith is what keeps us going, faith is what has us coming back to Scripture time and time again. And faith is what we see lived out over and over in the lives of the people around us.

By faith, Christy passed through the shadows of death valley, showing me that faith can conquer fears, that hope is far better than despair, that love is the greatest healer of all, that God's promises are kept, even beyond these days we call life.

By faith, Bob has gone into the fiery furnace of false accusations, unsubstantiated rumors, name-calling, and those people who hugged him as they slipped the knife into his back - and come out with a stronger resolve to continue to model the love of God, the grace of Jesus Christ, the gentle peace of the Spirit.

By faith, Teddy wakes up each morning, believing that today, and every day, something wonderful, something exciting, something new and different is going to take place in his life.

Time won't let me tell you of all the people I know like Teddy, Bob, and Christy. But I hope you will take the time to think of all those who, like these three, remind us of the simple truth that unravels all the complexities of life:

it all has to do with faith.

And what more should I say?

When we went to pick up Dusty the Church Dog, the family which was having to give him up for adoption gave us a laundry basket full of stuffed animals and other toys, a stand which held a water bowl and food dish, the dog food they had been feeding him, and a crate.

He has been crate-trained, they told us, which meant that when we left the house, he would go into the crate, let us shut the door on him, and leave him there while we were gone for whatever amount of time. He didn't mind it, we were assured, and was quite used to staying in the crate.

So, a few days later when we knew we would be away for a few hours, I took Dusty down the stairs to the bedroom where his crate was kept. I opened the door, and told him to go in, which he did. He sat down and watched me, with his big, brown, trusting eyes, as I closed the door to the crate. I told him we would be back in a few hours, turned, went up the few steps to the living room, and walked out the front door towards the car where Bonnie was waiting. Just as I reached the car, I realized I had left something in the house.

I turned, went back to the house, opened the front door and there was Dusty, sitting on the floor of the living room, right inside the door, watching me with his big, brown, trusting eyes.

I couldn't believe it! Thinking he had destroyed the crate, I rushed down to the bedroom, but there it was, still standing, still completely assembled, the door of the crate shut and latched. No indication that he had tipped it over, no bent bars that he had squeezed through, no evidence of how he had managed to get out.

Most of us try to keep God in a crate, telling the Divine to go inside, sit down, curl up and go to sleep while we go about with our lives. We'll come down with food and water, we'll take God out for a nice walk once in a while, we'll even spend some time tossing toys. But we expect God to be crate-trained, don't we?

Most of us like to keep Jesus as that little baby asleep in the tissue of Christmas, placing him in the nicest box, wrapping the shiny paper all around, and tying it off with a big bow before we put him on the shelf with the rest of the decorations.

We think if we keep the windows shut tight, with the latches locked; if we put deadbolts on all the outside doors and keep the keys hidden, if we alarm our house and never share the code with anyone, then there is absolutely no way the Spirit can sneak in and set those tongues of fire dancing on top of our heads and teach us those funny languages!

But we turn around and there they are, sitting and watching us with their big, brown, trusting eyes and (like Dusty) with just a hint of a smile tugging at their mouths.

I finally gave up trying to get Dusty to stay in the crate, and just let him be himself.

Maybe I should try that with the Three!

If I thought it would do any good, I would send the president of Iran a box of those hard, candy hearts to try to make amends.

I would send the members of Hamas a bouquet of daffodils to brighten their day and to let them know that I have no hard feelings towards them.

I would send cards with warm, generous words to all those Muslims throughout the world, to let them know that respect for others should be a guiding principle when it comes to exercising my freedoms.

I would send chocolate to all those people I may have offended, or hurt, or forgotten through all the years and who let me know that I have done so by the tone of their voices and the looks on their faces.

But it seems that there is just not anything, anyone, any group, any leader, any cleric, any nation can do to overcome the anger that so many people - so many of us - feel these days. From parents yelling at children, to children yelling at friends, to friends refusing to talk to one another; from horns blaring the instant the traffic light changes to garbage being thrown in a sports arena because of a call that went the way we didn't like to trashing embassies, we are an angry, angry world.

We're angry because our lives have not turned out the way we were told they would; we're angry because we work so hard, and our bosses don't appreciate our efforts and our families don't like our long hours; we're angry because we can't have what the person down the street has; we're angry at God because God doesn't give us what we want, or do as we ask, no matter how hard we pray.

And anger is so sweet, anger is so powerful, anger is so addictive, we would rather hold onto it, no matter how much it might destroy us. We may worry about cancer killing us, but anger surely will.

Unless . . .

. . . we can come to the One who teaches us to let go of anger, and to pick up gentleness in its place; unless we listen to the One who speaks to us of the blessing we will receive if we go and reconcile ourselves with our sisters and brothers, rather than continuing to rage against them; unless we follow the One who had every profanity hurled at him and spoke forgiveness; who was criticized by everyone around him and constantly invited them to experience God's unconditional love; unless we are willing to become as addicted to acts of mercy and grace as strongly as we are to being justified in our anger.

Unless we are willing to change our hearts, our lives, our way of being and doing; unless we are willing to become more loving and less angry; unless we are willing to be transformed by the amazing power of God's grace - why should anyone else listen to us?

duh!

At least once a day, hopefully twice, I put the collar on Dusty, hook him up to the leash, and step out the door to take a walk. We try to do 10k steps a day (btw, would that be 40k for him?) so we both lose weight. And, as I am getting him ready, I usually am figuring out what route we will take. Depending on the time we have, I have a 30 minute route, a 45 minute, and an hour I have 'plotted out' over the years.

So, as we walked out of the church the other day, I knew which way we would go. But Dusty would have none of it. At the very first corner, when I wanted to go straight, he insisted we would turn right, and the only reason he waited was for the lights to change. I wasn't in any sort of mood to argue, so I just followed along, figuring he had sniffed something in the air, which made him want to go that direction.

About a block and a half down the street, I discovered why Dusty wanted to go the way we did. A young mother was putting her toddler in his car seat, while holding her 14-15 month old in her other arm. When the older kid was strapped in, and she turned towards us, the little one in her arms got a big grin on his face, and began to wave.

Turns out he loves dogs, and when mom asked if he could say hello, Dusty immediately went up to the little guy (wobbling barefoot in the grass while clinging onto mom's hand), and gave him a big sloppy dog kiss. Pure delight filled the kid's face. As we said goodbye, and walked on down the street, I simply said to Dusty, "okay, I'll pay better attention to your prodding next time," and his look at me clearly said, "duh!"

Most days, I get up and put a leash on God, expecting the Holy One to simply heel, to trot obediently at my side, stopping when I want to stop, going where I want to go, speaking to who I want to speak, continuing to be that faithful, domesticated creature I want in my life.

But those moments when I let God take the lead, when I take the leash off and follow into the wonders of the world, when I meet the folks I need to meet, when I travel down those unfamiliar streets I haven't wandered before, when I pause long enough to take off my shoes and wander barefoot in the fields of the kingdom, it is pure delight.

And God's look at me, in such moments, clearly says, "Duh!"

Here at church, we're 'task-forcing' our Personnel Ministry: taking a look at the policies and practices, how we do (or should do) evaluations, job descriptions. It's something that every church does (or should) on a periodic basis. It's a good thing for us.

The job description of the pastor concerns me. In fact, it has in every church I have served. I think it's because so many job descriptions for pastors are based on some business model, with objectives, goals, evaluation tools, etc. These are not necessarily wrong; I happen to think they are inadequate for trying to describe (or evaluate) what a pastor does.

So many of these descriptions talk about being able to manage this or that task/person/board, administrative skills, judicatory roles, 'targets' to meet, constituencies to serve. Even the 21st-century 'model' we are exploring talks of 'abilities' to manage, promote, communicate, etc. Again, these are not necessarily bad, and if, as I suspect, my new job description ends up with such language, I can live with it.

Yet, I long for a description that reads something like this:

The role of the pastor is:
- to draw people to the wells of Living Water, where Jesus is waiting to chat with them;
- to sit with individuals as they go through their dark nights of the soul;
- to lead them to the refuge God provides for them in their wilderness wanderings;
- to steady people as they stand under God's Word and feel the Spirit transforming their lives;
- to pick up kids and place them on the lap of Jesus so he can bless them;

- to laugh with delight when folks take the training wheels
  off discipleship and shakily ride down the street
  after Jesus;
- to sweep up the crumbs from under the Table and
  remember that these are all we really need
  to have faith;
- to bandage the wounds from the hurts arc pains of
  the world;
- to live in relationship with the people with whom God
  has graced me, especially the ones who drive
  me crazy;
- to be a servant.

I've got a feeling such a job description would transform
me, as well as the church.

From the 3rd to the 8th grades, we lived in Arlington, Florida, a 'suburb' of Jacksonville. We lived on Ector Road, in a yellow house that was more than enough for a family of 7, with a big back yard. It was a time when all the houses in the neighborhood were filled with kids, and each yard had its own magical spots, for games, for hiding, for mystery.

We spent hours playing the outdoor games of the times: cowboys and indians, war, Davy Crockett, baseball, football. We rode our bicycles up and down the wide, sunny streets, dropping them in the yard of whatever house we decided to 'invade' next with our noise, fun, and laughter. Nearby was a small lake, surrounded by homes, but which was open to all for swimming, fishing, and playing. A long bike ride took us to the library, the store, the pharmacy with its comic books and soda fountain. It was a wonderful time and a marvelous place.

So, when Bonnie and I were in Florida to do a wedding one year, I decided I would show her the Elysian Fields where I had spent so many wonderful, happy hours. But the closer we got, and the remembered street names flashed by - the more unfamiliar the whole place looked! I thought I was lost.

Because in the last 50 years, someone had come in and narrowed all the streets; a scientist had used some sort of ray-gun on our house and shrunk it to half its original size; the houses had all been pushed closer together; the yards had all been reduced to about the size of a postage stamp - and there were no kids around, or at least none were outside on a beautiful fall afternoon.

Of course, none of it had really changed; I had. I was now seeing my neighborhood through the eyes of an adult, cynical and weary from all the years behind me, not the eyes of a little boy for whom everything was bigger and brighter, with his years ahead of him.

Maybe that's why Jesus tells us that if we want to see God's kingdom, God's neighborhood, God's future, we need to become little children again.

So we can see trees that are not dropping a big bunch of leaves we have to spend time raking up, but which are just right for climbing so we can touch the sky, and will provide just the right shade for reading a book on a summer's day.

So we can see streets that are not narrow and filled with too many parked cars, but those streets paved with the laughter of children, curbed with the joy of innocence, wide enough where we can all join hands for a game of 'red rover, red rover, send Jesus right over'.

So we can find houses where every door is open wide to welcome all of God's children, where the smell of bread just out of the oven fills the air, where we can grab the hose and get a drink of cool, refreshing living waters whenever we need them.

So we can find our way home again.

The little kids have left for the day, so now Dusty can come back to the office, do his 'circle dance' three times, give a big sigh, put his head on his paws, and sleep, for he's done his job.

When he is over here in the office, Dusty is responsible for making sure that the 3 and 4-year-olds who come to the nursery get in the building okay, and then leave for home in good spirits. He supervises them from the top of the landing and if, as usually happens, one of them spots him and wants to pet him, he is more than willing. Just the other day, he had 8 or 9 of them touching and loving him, smiling and laughing. It's hard, but hey, he figures someone has to do the dirty jobs in a church.

And when the lunch groups come in during the month, he is more than willing to put a smile on their faces, as he greets them and sits quietly, while they make a fuss over him.

So far, no one has 'accidently' dropped any food on the floor for him, but Dusty is very, very patient.

Unconditional love, patience, acceptance, coming and searching for me when I've left the room for more than 3 seconds, bounding up to me and jumping up to give me a kiss when he finds me - all are part of Dusty's character.

No wonder God spelled backwards is dog - they have a lot in common.

sightless

Someone asked me the other day about the 'absence' of gospel sightings the last few weeks.

Maybe it's because the doctor has discovered a cataract in my right eye, and that's why I am having trouble 'seeing' the gospel these days.

I could claim the 'excuse' of being too stressed out, overworked and underpaid, of being too fatigued. But that's all they are - excuses. Or maybe I am mad at God and I want a 'sign' not just some vague glimmer in the distance. But

in the woman who talked with me yesterday about her plan to fast and pray for our Session retreat scheduled for tomorrow;

in the children who stop to pet Dusty and look up at me with such pure delight in their eyes;

in the friends in England, Australia, New Zealand, and all the points in between who write to ask how Teddy, Bonnie, and I are doing;

in the staff at the Developmental Center who tell us how much they love Teddy and what a joy he is to work with;

in a thousand different moments from thousands of different people in each and every day:

the gospel keeps an eye on me, even when I remain stubbornly sightless.

As Dusty the Church Dog and I walked in the early morning moonlight, we passed a young boy sitting on the bench at the corner, waiting in the dusky darkness for the school bus to pick him up. As we turned and continued down the street, about 4 houses from the corner, we passed a woman standing at the end of her driveway. We said a good morning to each other, but her eyes never left the young man waiting at the corner. Just then, I heard the air brakes on the bus hiss as it stopped, and then it started on down the street. At that point, she smiled, whispering to herself "okay," and went back into her house to continue her day.

When we lay in the hospital bed, groggy and recovering from the surgery, or lying awake in the middle of the night staring at the ceiling wondering what word the doctor will bring when he makes his rounds, God is sitting in the corner, in that hard, uncomfortable chair (which could fold out into an even more painful bed if one chooses), keeping her eye on us, staying awake as long as we do, and even longer.

When we wander around the shelves in the always open store at the corner of Temptation and Wayward, finally going up to the counter to order one of those iced drinks filled to the brim with foolishness and wrong choices, Jesus paces back and forth outside on the sidewalk, pretending to search for change in the pay phone, looking for all the world as if he has nothing on his mind, just waiting to 'accidentally' bump into us as we walk out the door, knocking the drink out of our hands, letting it spill all over his front.

When the P. A. announces that the train is ready to board, we join the line, jostling and pushing, pulling our battered luggage on its rickety wheels, till we find our seat and wearily settle back for the ride, handing our ticket marked Anywhere But Here to the conductor. And as we are just about to fall asleep, thinking no one has noticed or cares, Sophia comes along with her cart, asking, "Something from the trolley, dearie?" as she hands us a loaf of bread and a bottle of wine.

Wherever, whenever, however God is always near.

A parishioner shared with me the remarks which David Stevens, Leader of the Corrymeela Community in Northern Ireland, made at the Service of Dedication this month. Here is part of what he said:

"There is a temptation or a tendency to look with morbid fascination at what has gone wrong, or what is going wrong. It's part of human life. And we in Corrymeela are no exception in this. There is the pleasant *schadenfreude* of watching things go wrong and there is the destructive tendency to encourage them to go wrong. Our personal negativity has a wish for general negativity."

In other words, if I am pessimistic (and part of a group), rather than letting the group lift my spirits or help change my attitude, I want the rest of the group to be pessimistic.

When I worked in a college setting, I saw how the constant, negative sniping by one or two members of the faculty and staff "wore down" the rest of us over time. In fund-raising, there is an "axiom" that 2% of people will always, always oppose any campaign, and most efforts fail because of the desire to get that 2% on board. In churches, most people leave, most conflict results, most pastors are "removed" not because of any one incident, sermon, or decision, but because of an undercurrent of negativity.

And, according to Stevens, it can even happen in the Corrymeela Community, a group committed to peace and reconciliation. It's all too true - group dynamics are often affected more by the negativity of a small percentage of people than all the positive outlooks of the majority.

So, what can a person, a group, a church do?

Not surprisingly, David Stevens turns to Scripture. He goes on to say, "When Peter tries to counteract human weakness with words of hope, he did not encourage people to say what was wrong with the world, the church, or society. He did not ask people to draw up a list of problems or negatives. Instead he asks them simply to give an account of the hope that is in them: ' . . . explain the hope you have in you.' (1 Peter 3:15)"

Explain the hope you have in you - talk about why you are a church member, or a teacher, or a police officer; tell stories of what you see as you walk your child to school, as you ride the bus to work, as you sit in the shade on a summer's day; write a short story about the person who rescued you when you had fallen into despair's grasp; craft a poem about the teacher who patiently worked with you until you understood fractions; sing a song about that special place where you can stand silent, vulnerable, obedient to God.

And don't just explain - live out that hope you have in you. Have an honest conversation with the neighbor who troubles you; pray about that decision you wish you didn't have to make; learn a new language so you can welcome the immigrants who are moving into your community; make a pilgrimage of trust to the refuge God provides for you, and then go back home, a changed person.

Take that hope you have in you - even if it is buried so deep inside of you that you are not aware of it - and offer it as a fragrant offering to everyone around you. Because if you do, then slowly, tentatively, gently, joyfully, they will begin to share that hope they have deep within themselves.

And no one will be the same any more.

Another family, another church, another rejection.

Bonnie got a call last night from a member of the support group for folks who have a family member who has Fetal Alcohol Related Birth Defects. The mother is used to dealing with neighbors who don't understand; with teachers who are not sure what to do with her son; with case workers who have to be 'trained' by the family on how to provide the services needed for their loved one.

But the church?

Her son, like many folks with FARBD, has trouble with focusing and being attentive, with sitting for very long periods of time, with being able to do all the 'normal' things that a person his age can do. So, over the years, instead of being in worship, he sat in a classroom with other kids, just scribbling and writing and drawing on paper. Not bothering the other kids, not touching them, not being in the way - just sitting there doing his "paperwork" - in a place where God was, where God's love could be found, where he could find a family. Or so he and his mother had been told.

But now, the decision has been made that he should not be 'doing' whatever he does in the classroom. He 'should' be in the sanctuary with his mother, he 'should' be sitting quietly and attentively, he 'should' not get up and wander around. And his mother, because she has heard all the other stories from all the other families in the support group about their experiences with church, knows this is the first step the church is taking in getting them to leave.

"Oh no," you will say, "that's not what is meant. This is not what the leadership of the church is saying." And I will simply tell you of the dozens of calls I have gotten (because I am both a pastor and a parent of a child with FARBD as well as other disabilities) that this is how folks who have family members with profound disabilities are treated by the church.

All these folks are doing is looking for a place where they are accepted for who they are, not judged for who they cannot be; a place where they are loved because they are differently-gifted, not ridiculed because they are not bright and healthy; where they are affirmed as one of God's children, not condemned because of something someone must have done that was contrary to God's will.

And once again, as I always do after I hear such sad stories from families who have not only unconditional love for their child, but also an unshakeable faith in God, I wished that I was independently wealthy, so I could go rent a storefront somewhere and start the "Church for the broken, the rejected, the least, the lost, the little, the ridiculed, the hurt."

But isn't that what Jesus tried to start?

Dusty, the Golden Retriever who goes by the various names of Church Dog, Assistant Pastor, First Greeter, or Furry Caregiver, is spending the summer at home with my wife who is off these three months from school.

Otherwise, he would be 'parked' outside my door, ready to greet whoever walks through the door, ready to put a smile of someone's face, ready to reluctantly <g> receive a pat, a hug, a belly rub from all ages, all sizes, all personalities.

He is somewhat depressed lately, because the nursery school is closed for the summer, so there are no little kids who look for him when they come through the front door. But he loves it when he gets to lead me around the neighborhood, and inevitably, some little kid will run up and say 'hello' or tell their parents or siblings, "There's Dusty from church!"

He once attended our 11 p.m. Christmas Eve service, lying quietly and calmly in the narthex, keeping watch over the ceramic figures in the crèche, while we sang, prayed, and welcomed the Christ Child into our hearts once again. And then, he joined me in greeting folks and wagging them a most "Merry Christmas!"

While I am sure that there are those who grumble about the pastor's dog in the church, I now know there would be more folks who would grumble if they came hoping to see Dusty, and he was no longer 'welcome' at the church. I know all about the worries about insurance, about kids and people who are frightened of dogs (and knowing them as I do, I make sure they do not encounter Dusty), about dogs around little kids.

I also know the studies of how people's blood
pressure drops when around dogs and cats, and know
that any church can use some dropping of its BP; I know
of the research of how therapeutic animals can be for
people, and I see how petting a dog, or having a cat on
one's lap while you are having a conversation causes a
different 'tone'; I have seen frowns changed into smiles;
complaints turned into laughter; curmudgeons turned into
marshmallows, all because of a goofy dog.

Animals in church? Of course.

And St. Francis would bless every single one of us for
such inclusionary love.

THAT anniversary is back.

It was on a cold, blustery, November day all those years ago, that the wire services carried the news of the his death. It was a word we had not expected to hear, hoping against hope that somehow, in some way, the press had gotten it wrong.

It was too soon for him to be taken away from us. He still had things to do, words to share with us, visions with which to inspire us, thoughts and hopes and dreams all contained within him, just waiting to be shared. It felt like, at least to me, that I was just starting to learn from him, I was just starting to be energized by him, I was just starting to understand what it was that he believed and lived and yearned for.

And then, he was gone. Just like that.

Yet, even after all these years, his words continue to be poured over by countless millions throughout the world. His life has inspired books, movies, TV shows. His thoughts and beliefs are analyzed by students in classrooms from the States to Australia and all the points in between. His vision of what the world could be - of what we could be - still is as relevant, and powerful, and needed as it was all those years ago. Just in the last few years, a whole new generation has been introduced to him.

I am one of those who still talks about him, still remembers him, still reads him. In fact, just about a month ago, I quoted him (once again) in a sermon, reminding folks of what he had to say about giving:

"Charity - giving to the poor - is an essential part of Christian morality. I do not believe one can settle how much we ought to give. I am afraid the only safe rule is to give more than we can spare. In other words, if our expenditure on comforts, luxuries, amusements, etc. is up to the standard common among those with the same income as our own, we are probably giving away too little. If our charities do not at all pinch or hamper us, I should say they are too small. There ought to be things we should like to do but cannot because our charitable expenditure excludes them."

It was on a cold, blustery November day that the news came that Clive Staples Lewis died.

And we still miss him.

Some came, proudly toting the book bag that was almost as big as they are. Others came, huddling behind Dad's leg, staring in silence at the big people in the room. A few came with tears running down their faces, a few clutching tightly to Mom's hand or the stuffed animal which had slept with them last night.

The 3-year-olds showed up for their first day at the nursery school housed in the rooms underneath my office. They came with wonder on their faces, with breakfast still on their lips, with just a little bit of fear in their eyes.

We all know about fear, don't we? So, we can imagine and empathize with the fears some of these kids carried with them as they got out of the security of the booster seat in the car and tiptoed towards the front door of the church.

We all know about fear because we remember our first day at school, our first day at practice, our first day at work, our first day as a newlywed, our first day as a parent. We know about fear because we continue to look at our aging face in the mirror each morning, as we go to our doctor's office to hear the results of tests, as we see images from September 11th and New Orleans replayed over and over on TV.

And, we know about fear because as people of faith, our book - the Bible - is filled with stories of fearful people.

Imagine the fear of Sarah and Abraham as they are instructed by God to leave the retirement village and begin a new life. Imagine the fear of the Israelites in Egypt who, though shackled by slavery, were asked to embark on a journey into that wilderness called the future. Imagine the fear of a young girl visited by an angel and told she would bear God's child. Imagine the fear of that outsider - by gender, by race, by geography - who asked for help from Jesus for her daughter, even if all he had to offer were the left-overs from the miracles in his pocket.

Imagine that fear, as you think of your own.

How did they do it? Were they smarter than me; holier than you - how did they do what we are told they did in scripture?

Maybe it was because in the midst of their fears, even those which were far greater than anything they had imagined, they heard God's 11th commandment: Do Not Fear!

It's that scarlet thread that is woven throughout the tapestry of our relationship with God. From God's assurance to creation that all was good, to a woman praying in the temple for a child; from Hosea's reminder that God will not abandon us, to Isaiah's vision of God fixing the road to our hearts; from Mary's great song of redemption for those favored least by the world, to John's vision of the Holy City whose gates are not closed to anyone, God cajoles, encourages, begs, and pleads with us to not let our fears run or ruin or lives.

Whatever the circumstance, wherever we may go, whoever we might encounter, God is with us. We can hide behind God's leg when our fears make us shy, we can cling to God's hands when our fears make us nervous, we can feel God's fingers wiping away our tears when our fears make us weep. We can let go of our fears and hand them to God to keep for us, as we step forward into that kingdom in which we are invited to live.

Fear not!

Right up front, let's be clear. God did not will what happened at Dunblane, Virginia Tech, Mumbai, or Newtown. Period.

I have said, as I have done when such things happen, that for some impossible-to-understand, mysterious, divine reason, God "allowed" it to happen. So, why do I get such a sour taste in my mouth when I say those words? If God is the sort who would "allow" people to be slaughtered in what most assume to be a very safe, and normally serene, environment, then I wonder if I want to continue to believe in such a God.

Then, I look at the culture in which I live. A culture which idolizes guns and violence. A culture which puts anger up on a pedestal and doesn't dare knock it off. A culture which gives assent to the notion that we can carry around our grudges as long as we want, and act on them whenever, wherever we want. A culture in which every form of media is obsessed with death, with killing, with brutality. (And don't think that the church is free of such a culture, of such dark emotions. Demonization and vilification of those who disagree with us is standard practice.)

By my watching such movies, and reading such books, and playing such video games I acquiesce to this culture. By my silence, I encourage the culture to continue on this now-beyond-reckless course. By my silence, I allow these things to take place.

So, maybe it is the other way around. Maybe God wonders about continuing to believe in me, about believing in us, about believing in those who have been created in the divine image.

Yet, the evidence is there that even if this is what God is wondering, God chooses to be involved with us. We see it in the flood of helpers who show up at those places, on those days, and those tomorrows, and beyond - the grief counselors, the therapists, the religious leaders, the doctors, the nurses - to bring healing and hope to a devastated community. And long after the anchors, and the TV crews, and the reporters have packed up their equipment and gone on to the next story, they will still be there.

I do not believe that what happens at places like Dunblane, Virginia Tech, Mumbai, or Newtown is God's will. But I do believe that God wills healing, wholeness, and new life for all those shattered by this tragedies. I do believe God wills that the helpers will never, ever have to respond to another crisis like this.

And I do believe God wills that the silence stops.

It was one of those questions authors are sometimes asked to provide to become more personal/human to readers. Are you a dog person or a cat?

For over 50 years, I was a cat person. I love cats, and they seemed to love me (or at least as much as cats can 'love' such an inferior being!). I always had at least one cat around me, and it seemed that every stray within 20 miles would find its way to my door.

Then, in 2003, we got our first canine, Cocoa the Wonder Dog. Elsewhere, I have talked about how she got us through Teddy's cancer, and how she graced our life. Now, Dusty the Church Dog, continues to do the same.

And over the last few years, I have discovered that dogs are that very visible sign of that presence we cannot see called God.

It doesn't matter what time I go home, Dusty is waiting to greet me. And not just waiting, he is thrilled that I am home. Whether he is standing with his paws against the front window, looking out as I get out of my truck, or spinning in circles, with a goofy stuffed toy in his mouth, I am greeted as if I am the prodigal returning home from years of slopping the pigs. No wonder Jesus tells that story about how God waits to greet us.

Dusty just loves walking with me. He is constantly turning around, looking at me, as if to say, "See how much fun this is? Let's do this forever!"

It doesn't matter what the weather is – mushing through 6 inches of snow, slipping on the ice, trudging through rain that soaks your soul, or sweating through those dog days of August, Dusty is ready to go with me. God makes me the same promise.

And when I am feeling so low I can't see bottom, Dusty comes up and puts his head in my lap and looks at me with loving eyes. When I feel like I don't have a friend in the world and want to just hide under the covers, Dusty jumps up in the bed and curls up next to me. When all I can see is the grayness and gloom of the world, Dusty drags me outside and points me to the squirrels racing up and down the tress, the leaves playing hopscotch down the sidewalk, the kids going to the stars in an empty refrigerator box.

And the Spirit takes a deep breath in my soul.

Just then a Pope stood up to test Jesus. "Master," he said, "what must I do to belong to the true church?" Jesus said to him, "What does the Bible say? What do you read there?" He answered, "You shall love the Lord your God with all that you are and all that you have; and you shall welcome and embrace your neighbor as you would yourself." And Jesus said, "Right on! You've read the words, now if you live them out, you are part of the household of God."

But wanting to justify himself, and his teachings, he asked Jesus, "Who is my neighbor?" Jesus replied, "Let me tell you a story."

A man was going from Vatican City down to visit the Coliseum, and a gang of kids cornered him in an alley, knocked him around a few times, took all his cash, credit cards, and smart phone, and left him lying next to a dumpster.

Now by chance, a Cardinal was walking by chatting on his cell phone to a journalist, about the latest papal edict. When he saw the man lying in the alley, he blinked and then crossed to the other side to get better reception. A few minutes later, a priest came by, trying to memorize the Latin Rite for the Mass. He went into the alley to take a short cut, but turned back when he saw the fellow next to the garbage.

But a group of tourists came walking by, and one of them, a Baptist, glancing down the alley, saw the man and was moved with pity. He went to him, sat him up, wiped the blood off his face, and gave him some of his water. He helped him to his feet, and went to the street, where he flagged down a taxi. Going to his hotel, he got a room for the man, and got his doctor friend from back home (who was also on the tour) who checked the injured man out and said all he needed was some rest.

The next day, the tour group was checking out to go visit Tuscany for a few days. The Baptist went to the front desk, gave the manager his credit information, and said, 'We'll be back in three days. Please make sure my friend gets whatever he needs, and just put it on my card."

"So, what do you think?" Jesus asked. "Which of the three showed they belonged to the 'true' church (whatever in the world that is)?"

Looking down at his shoes, the Pope replied, "The one who did what you would have done."

"You got it," said Jesus.

sprung

This morning, Dusty the Church Dog, went out in the back yard, sat down in the grass, stuck his nose up into the air, sniffed, nodded his head at the fresh smells, and then proceeded to roll around in pure delight on the grass. So now it is official:

the first day of spring is here!

The birds, which the day before seemed to huddle against the chill wind without a peep between them, have been rehearsing all morning for the Easter cantata.

The squirrels, which wouldn't venture further than a foot from the base of their favorite oak tree, are now chasing each other from yard to yard, and tree to tree, like children playing tag.

The flowers, which peeked their heads out of the ground a few weeks ago and then quickly ducked back in, are now boldly reaching for the warmth of the sun, giving us glimpses of glory that will soon be in full array.

The grass, which has been that ugly shade of dead-brown we see every winter, is teasing us with those shadings of green that always seem to catch us by surprise each year.

And the clouds are flexing their muscles, as they drift slowly across the sky, shaping and reshaping themselves as if to challenge us to lay on our backs and guess who or what they look like now.

It's the first day of spring.

Did you notice?

He starts out at the end of the sofa, head erect, gaze firmly looking out the living room window. As the evening wears on, the dusk darkens, and the lights in the houses around us come on, he begins to grow just a little weary, sometimes resting his head on the tray table, sometimes just 'resting' his eyes.

But he will wait, for however long it takes for that is his job.

Then, before any other ears can hear anything, his head snaps up and his eyes are wide and wonderful. Jumping to look out the front window, his joy and eagerness begin to bubble.

Forget the ring and the best robe, he races around trying to decide which stuffed animal he will carry as he bounds out the door to greet the prodigal who has returned – from her book club, her volunteering, her evening at the ice cream parlor with a friend.

And with a leap and a look that says 'get out of my way,' as I throw open the front door, Dusty races out of the house to run up to the car before it has come to a complete stop and welcome the wanderer home.

Jesus tells us stories about a lost sheep, a lost coin, and about the father who sits up each night, looking down the road, waiting, waiting, waiting for the wayward son to come home. It is one of the most cherished stories in our faith tradition, a story of hope and reconciliation, a parable about how God waits and waits, longs and longs for us. And Jesus says there is great joy in heaven over the one who was lost and has been found.

But it can't be any greater than the joy Dusty has when his beloved Bonnie comes home!

Yesterday, in church, the Epistle lesson was the one from Philippians 3:4b-14, where Paul says "Yet whatever gains I had, these I have come to regard as loss because of Christ. More than that, I regard everything as loss because of the surpassing value of knowing Christ Jesus my Lord."

Growing up in a region and time in which there were always revivals taking place, especially in the summer, I knew of a lot of folks who were willing to give up the worst of their lives - drinking, gambling, affairs, etc. - for Christ. But I don't recall a single person coming forward to give up their law practice, or big house, or Cadillac in order to follow Jesus.

So I wanted to give a visual lesson to the kids about what Paul was talking about. I brought in a trash can, and asked about what we use it for. "Trash," was the spoken answer. "duh" was the look on their faces. So, we put some trash in the can. I mentioned what Paul said, about tossing his 'gains,' those things of value, into the trash can.

To demonstrate this, I took out, showed the kids, and talked about the meaning of the chipped and cracked communion cup with which Bonnie and I and the rest of the wedding party had celebrated the Lord's Supper at our rehearsal dinner so many years ago . Then I put it in the trash can.

Next, I took the souvenir cup from the very first Cincinnati Reds ball game I ever attended when we moved here - the 1st game of the 1990 World Series. And it went into the trash. It was followed by the card given to me each year which says I am a minister member in good standing in the PCUSA.

Finally, I showed the kids my diplomas from both college and seminary. I earned the first through ten years of struggle. The second came at the cost of having to learn two other languages, when I have enough trouble with English. These ended up in the 'round file' as well.

By now, the kids were edging away from me, and looking at me as if I had completely lost it. Then we had the prayer and sang a hymn and went on with the service. I was feeling pretty good about how that time with the kids went (and how it certainly said something to all the 'big kids' as well!).

Until I went home.

"Well, did you get all that stuff out of the trash can after worship?" Bonnie asked me. "Of course," I replied, looking at her as if she had completely lost it.

"Oh, so it was just an 'object lesson' for the kids, and not something you really believe," was her comment, before continuing to put away the groceries.

One of my favorite detective/mystery authors is Anne Perry. I have recently finished her newest series set in World War I, with much of the action, mystery and war, taking part on the front lines. Her descriptions of the horrors of that time, of the trench warfare, of the terrible rains and flooding which caused many soldiers to literally drown in the mud, are heart-wrenching. One wonders how anyone could keep their sanity, their perspective, their faith.

Last week, I discovered that one of the ways in which some of them tried to 'keep it together' was through gardening. Several months ago, a great friend gave me a copy of a book called "Defiant Gardens: Making Gardens in Wartime." The author, Kenneth I. Helphand, has discovered that in the midst of extreme social, economic, political conditions, people respond by creating gardens.

In the midst of trenches dug deep into the earth and forests decimated by shelling, troops in World War I (on both sides) built gardens, floral and vegetable, near their trenches, their shelters, their dugouts. Surrounded by a vision of hell, they tried to recreate memories, smells, and tastes of home. In the Warsaw ghetto of World War II, in the prisoner of war camps, in the relocation camps for Japanese-Americans, in the concentration camps, people defiantly gardened. They would not let death, or fear, or the unknown future deter them from being reminded of new life, new hope.

I remember when I was in Europe on my renewal time and seeing the flowers and plants growing in the cracks of the ruins of the nunnery on Iona, and the abbey at Cluny. I remember walking through Oban and seeing daffodils and tulips defiantly standing tall in the face of cold, cold winds. I remember seeing homes in dirty, grimy, low-income areas, whose yards were ablaze with bright flowers and blooming trees.

Of course, we have been taught well by One who knows a little bit about gardening (and defiance).

The One who will sprinkle dandelions right in the midst of the award-winning lawn we are trying to create. The One who creates plants which can withstand the complete lack of attention that someone like me will give them if they dare enter my life. The One who places seeds under concrete parking lots and massive boulders, and laughs when trees burst out of such tombs.

In the midst of our struggles, our losses, our doubts, our worries, the Master Gardener invites us to be defiant in the face of all those people, all those events, all those terrors, all those moments which try to make our lives hell.

Now, where did I leave the packet of wildflower seeds?

"Is it inappropriate to ask for prayers for my kitty?" the email read.

At one point in my ministerial life, I probably would have answered in the affirmative. After all (I thought back then), God has too many things to worry about - important things like human suffering, like wars, like poverty, like hunger. All those abstract sorts of things that we are able to convince ourselves are the sole focus of God and God's interests.

But I've traveled too many miles down that road called discipleship, I've spent too many hours reading that strange book called the Bible, I've had Jesus by my side too long with all his whispers, his comments, his stories in my ears to think that way anymore.

Because I've learned that the Bible is not interested in abstract thoughts and concepts. It's interested in God's dreams, hopes, purposes for us, and how we will respond, how we will remain faithful, our struggles to be obedient.

God doesn't talk about suffering in general terms, God sees the suffering of specific people in places like Egypt and Babylon. God doesn't look at the poor as some 'class' of people for politicians to use as fodder for political salvos, God sees the poor as individuals we harm by our greed, by our unethical practices, by our inability to see them in our neighborhoods. God doesn't see the hungry and hope that some government agency steps forward to create a program to assist them. God tells them to sit down and turns to us, saying, "You give them something to eat."

God is involved - passionately, hopefully, persistently, patiently - in our lives. In every moment, in every situation, in everything we face and deal with.

So, I've got a feeling that the One whose eye is on the sparrow also is watching the cat that 'staks' it from inside a house, a cat named Sam, who has brought so much comfort, so much joy, so much grace to the young woman who has been his companion for 17 years.

Well, do you feel any better?" asked Bonnie as we
walked to the car. "Oh yeah!" I replied. "That was a
great movie; I'm so glad we saw it; I think the youth group
should go see it!" "No," she said, "do you feel any better
after what you did today?"

Do I feel any better after what I did (now yesterday)? I'm
not sure. I wasn't sure when I did it; I wasn't sure when
she asked me that question; I'm still not sure as I
reflect on it.

What did I do? I mailed some handwritten notes to the
folks in the church with whom I live in brokenness. I don't
think I did it in hopes that the sniping at me would end;
and I have to admit I didn't do it with great joy; and I
certainly didn't do it because it was my idea. I did it for
the simple reason that I kept being 'pushed' by God.

God works on me through one of the few true saints I
have met in my life, and who is a member of this church.
I have learned over the years to pay particular attention to
those moments when she says, "I think . . . I had a
thought . . . I dreamed . . ." Because it has turned out
that God was behind those thoughts, those ideas, those
dreams.

Not that I respond to those thoughts with eager
anticipation; not that I immediately jump into action when
God suggests something. After all, a lot of times, I am
being directed to do something that goes against my
human nature. To go see someone I'd rather avoid; to
listen patiently and quietly to someone who is going to
take another opportunity to tell me of my failures; to put
down that grudge that fits so comfortably into my pocket,
where I can touch it for its comfort whenever I need.

Like most folks I interact with, I am torn. I know that I should say to folks (far more often than I do) that if I have hurt them in any way, I hope they forgive me. I know that I don't say often enough (especially to the folks I care most about) 'I'm sorry." I know that I am supposed to do all that cheek turning, and extra miles walking, and coat sharing. I know, because that is what God asks me to do, and models for me in Jesus.

But, like most folks I know, I am human enough to wonder when it will be my turn: when do I get the apologies for the guff I have taken over the years; when does someone tell me they are sorry for the way they treated me, or a member of my family; when do I get the handwritten note? Not very Christ-like, but awfully Thom-like.

Maybe that's why the gospels have Jesus growing up so quickly. He's being born one moment, circumcised the next, in the Temple trying to teach the elders what's going on, and then getting baptized and sent out into the world. He's sent out to talk with those folks who are determined to criticize everything he says; he works with folks who nitpick everything he does; he is asked to set down all the hurts, the snide remarks, the angry looks as he continues to try to journey faithfully with God.

And all along the way, there are those surrounding him: 'have mercy', they cry; 'heal me,' they implore; 'come to my house and eat,' they invite; 'give me some of the crumbs off your table,' they challenge. All those ways, all those people, all those words (it seems to me) God used to nudge Jesus towards faithful obedience, turning from his human nature to that childlike nature of trust and faith - as uncomfortable, and frustrating, and irritating as it must have been at times.

Do I feel any better? I'm still not sure. But I do know that I don't want to stop feeling those nudges.

walls

The 'wallpaper' on my computer screen is a picture of Iona Abbey which I took years ago. The sky is blue, with white clouds brushed gently across it. The water in the sound is stirred just a little bit; the stones are roughened by the winds, worn smooth by memories of all the people who touched them, faded from all the love of Columba and the pilgrims who followed. The silence that day was a gentle embrace from God, deepening that moment.

After the morning service that day, I had sat for a long time in one of the choir stalls, waiting until the last footstep had echoed away, until the last whispered voice had wandered off, until the notes of the last hymn had floated away to heaven.

In the stillness, just staring at the stone walls, I thought of how many voices had been lifted in that place, how many times believers had gathered together over the centuries, all differences set aside for the sake of the oneness they had in God. I thought of all the chants and songs that had echoed back and forth, from stall to stall, from wall to wall; how many prayers had been flung upwards toward God, and whispered into the hollows of the hearts of the supplicants. I was just one pilgrim in a long line which stretched so far back into the past that the years blurred the very beginning, and which would stretch into that future cradled in God's imagination and joy.

Those walls were wailing walls – the repositories of the fears and failures, the hopes and hauntings, the tears and the torments, the joys and the jealousies, the longings and the lives of so many people. The stones were the silent witness of the faithfulness, as well as the foolishness, of people who came as pilgrims to that thin place and left, to continue their journeys in all those parts where life was tangled, thick, troublesome, hopeful.

And in the place where I will worship tomorrow, or next week, or next year, I will find more wailing walls. Some old and roughened, some fresh and smooth, glistening with new paint. Some will be shadowed with ancient longings and failed dreams, with windows stained with the detritus of despair; some will be bright, with sunlight streaming through crystal clear glass.

But they will listen - to our songs and prayers, our whispers and our longings, our aches and our joys. They will take what they have heard, cradle them, and offer them to the Holy Spirit, who will set them afire with her tears, offering them as sweet incense to our God.

According to some, this Latin phrase is one which the great artist, Michelangelo, spoke often during his life, even more so as he grew older. It translates as 'I am still learning.' Think about that. Someone as gifted, as creative, as intuitive as the guy who painted a ceiling that still attracts hundreds of thousands of tourists and carved statues that cause people to come to a complete halt to stand in a silence that stretches through the ages - he could say that he was still learning.

Now, I try to do crosswords, sudoku, word puzzles, brain teasers, all those sorts of things that are supposed to keep your mind sharp and, perhaps, ward off things like Alzheimer's. But sometimes I think I do them, not for the learning that comes from it, but because like any sort of 'exercise,' I need to do it on a regular basis.

But it's not just words or numbers that teach me. It's people!

There's the little girl Dusty and I pass on our morning walks. Standing on the corner waiting for her bus, she always has a smile of delight on her face, no matter what the weather might be. It is almost as if she knows, beyond any doubt, that something absolutely and incredibly surprising is going to happen to her on this very day, and she can hardly wait for it to show up in her life.

There is the much older woman who knows that she is on the last few miles of her journey through this world. Yet rather than living in the past, she looks forward to tomorrow and the chance she will have to visit a neighbor in the nursing unit. Rather than reflecting on all her struggles, she opens her life to share her story of faith and hope with the young man delivering her oxygen supply. Rather than whining about how hard it is to be old, she pours out the love and grace which is overflowing from her heart.

There's the father I watch from the porch, patiently and tenderly helping his child to learn how to ride the bike with the training wheels.   Walking beside her as she wobbles down the sidewalk, he guides her with a hand on the back, an encouraging nod, the word whispered in the ear, the smile that says 'you did it!' when she stops after 10 feet and turns her head up towards him.

God provides me with a lot of teachers throughout my life.

Am I still learning?

It wouldn't win any art awards. It wouldn't go for much on ebay or any of those online auction places. But every year, on Valentine's Day, Bonnie hangs it around her neck and wears it through the day.

It's a little ceramic heart, on a red ribbon, that simply says "Love" on it. It was Teddy's Valentine's Day gift to Bonnie over 20 years ago, when he 'made' it at the special school he attended when we were in Virginia.

Given before our hearts ached over his damaged life; given before our hearts would yearn for a healing which will never come; given before our hearts were broken over and over by the circumstances of his life; given before I thought we might lose the most tender heart I have ever known through his cancer, that little ceramic heart is a reminder of that Love God has poured into us

. . . that Love which might be chipped by the nicks and hammer blows of life, but which is constantly being repaired by grace . . .

. . . that Love which might fade in the long nights and shorter days of fear, worry, and doubt, but which is renewed through God's hope . . .

. . . that Love which might be hidden away in the recessed corners of that jewelry box we call life, but which will always find us when we least expect it . . .

. . . that Love which God has written upon our hearts, written in God's own hand, written in the promise which will never be broken.

It wouldn't win any art awards. It wouldn't go for much on ebay or any of those online auction places.

But it may be the most precious piece of jewelry we own.

The "Dog Whisperer," Cesar Millan, talks about how our lives could be better if we just modeled what we see dogs do.

For a dog, every morning is Christmas morning. I hear the alarm go off, mumble and fumble my way from under the covers, feeling around on the floor for my shoes, but Dusty the Church Dog is rarin' to go! He never met a morning he didn't like. It doesn't matter if it is still dark outside, or if the sun has been up for a while. He wants to get out to greet the world, to let the world know he is awake and ready to take it on for the day.

For a dog, every day is the best day of their life. I open my eyes instantly remembering what yesterday was like, and fretting that today might be even worse; I try to shake off those worry-induced dreams from the night before, hoping that they won't come true today. But for Dusty, it doesn't matter if it is hot outside, or cold, or snowy (in fact, the colder and snowier it is, the better he likes it - though if the precipitation is wet, not white, he can put off 'doing his business' for a while). It doesn't matter if yesterday was a hard one, or too long, or too tiring, or too anything. Today, this day, is brand new and just waiting to be explored.

For a dog, every walk is the best walk of their life. This morning, when I took Dusty out, we ended up (since I am the one at the 'controls') pretty much following the same path we took yesterday. Didn't matter one bit. That tree he sniffed at yesterday had brand new smells this morning; that squirrel that ran away from him yesterday almost got caught today; that little yippee dog that barked at him from its living room yesterday had another fit of jealousy when Dusty sauntered by, out for his morning constitutional. And the geese, the mist on the grass at the elementary school, the leaves drifting slowly down from the trees? It was as if he had never seen any of that before, he was so eager to take it all in.

For a dog, every meal is the best meal of their life. I open up that box of Cheerios, pouring in the same amount that I did yesterday and the day before, on top of the same sort of fruit that I used last week, drinking my tea from the same mug I always use, with the same amount of sweetener, and wearily park myself in the chair to watch the same weary news. But Dusty? He spins round and round, leaping high off the ground, his tongue falling out of his mouth, his eyes popping out of his head. And when I pour his food in the dish (the same food he eats morning after morning, just like I do), he looks at it with such pure delight, chuckles a big laugh, and digs in!

I wonder what my life would be like if I was able to treat every day as if it were the best day of my life and the one I have been longing to embrace and live; f I could start each morning, rarin' to go; if I could joyously sit down to breakfast, laughingly giving thanks to God for such wonder; if I could leave the house with my head held high, ready to go down that same old path I do every day, and come running back home at the end of my journey.

Maybe a dog's life is what God wishes for us!

The Cracker Lady died this morning. She went by so many names in her life - sister, wife, aunt, neighbor, mentor, Inez, Granny, and so many others (she even would identify herself as the 'pest' when she called me) - but over the last few years, that's how I knew her.

We would load up Dusty in the car and take him over to her apartment in the retirement center for a visit. At a certain point, he would know exactly where he was going, sticking his head out, the fur flying, the tongue drooling in anticipation. When we walked into the lobby, he would drag us over to the elevator, and when we got to her floor, he would practically drag us to her door, knowing from that incredible memory of his where it was, even if we seemed to be lost.

He would practically run into the room, but then would sit and stare at Inez, in her seat or in her wheelchair, his eyes starting to gleam, the anticipation rippling through his body, his butt hardly able to stay on the floor. He would put up with a certain amount of conversation among the people in the room, but eventually, he would lift his paw, and place it on her knee, letting her know that it was time to play their game.

And so, she would reach into her cache on the table next to her, keeping an eye on Dusty, telling him to sit, to behave, mind his manners (using that voice that would make a grown man buckle his knees in obedience), and then she would slip one edge of the cracker between her lips and lean towards him, as Dusty ever-so-gently (and ever-so-politely containing his eagerness) stretched his head towards her, and took the outer edge of the cracker in his mouth, and as she let go, he chewed and swallowed. I am not sure which one had more of a look of delight on their faces, but as I watched, I found myself in that thin place where steadfast love and mercy meet, where peace and righteousness kiss, where wonder and joy hold hands and giggle until they are exhausted.

So, you will forgive Dusty if he is not wagging his tail, or bouncing high in the air, or eager to go out to run. He'd rather just lay there, with his head on his paws, looking out the door on this gray, gloomy, rainy day . . .

. . . remembering, and missing, his beloved friend.

If Jesus had chosen 12 Golden Retrievers to follow him, instead of those yahoos he did choose, the end might not have been so rough. After all, Goldens wouldn't have betrayed or denied him, and they certainly would never abandon him. They would have been there at the foot of the cross; they would have followed him into the depths of hell; they would have kept an unceasing vigil at the tomb, waiting for the promises he had made to them to happen.

Every time I pull up to the house and see Dusty sitting there at the window waiting, and then racing to greet me as I come up the drive, I am reminded of the father of the prodigal, and understand more profoundly the incredible unconditional love God has for us.

When I watch him interact with the preschoolers when we go to read to them, letting them touch him, tug his ears, rub his paws, lean their heads against his, I hear Jesus inviting the little children to come to him, to be blessed with gentleness and acceptance.

When I see him go up to the woman we have met in the neighborhood who recently lost her own Golden and nudge her hand with his nose; when I see his brown eyes sparkle with delight at the elderly woman who always has biscuits for him down at the park; when I see him lie down at the feet of the person who has come into me to talk about the pain in his life, close enough to be touched if needed - I see lived out all those stories of how Jesus instinctively seemed to know what each person he met needed.

Each day, it seems, I get to 'read' the Gospel According to Dusty, and have my life enriched.

So, happy birthday today, Dusty! Thanks for being such an important part of my life.

vocatus atque non vocatus deus aderit

I've checked into Motel Stupid so many times in my life, tossing and turning on its hair shirt bed. Yet every morning, you are there, straightening up the room, putting out clean linen, hanging up my clothes, wanting to know if there is anything else you can do for me.

I've found myself in the crushing crowd at the Chaos concert, pushed and pulled and pummeled by the fears, doubts, and worries all around me. And I feel your hand on my shoulder, as you whisper in my ear 'I've got your back.'

I've bellied up to the bar at the Pub of Bad Choices, where you wipe off the bar with your veronica towel, top off my pint, hand it to me, and lean on your elbows asking, 'so, what brings you here tonight?'

Packed and finally ready to go, I take the last train to nowhere, hopping off and walking the last few yards to the edge of despair, where you stand looking over, shaking your head and muttering to yourself 'looks like a long drop to the bottom' as you shine your light for me, to show me a different path.

Over the entrance to his house in Zurich, and on his tombstone, psychologist Carl Jung had inscribed 'Vocatus atque non vocatus deus aderit.'

"Bidden or not bidden, God is present."

I was not looking forward to church this morning. Since the congregation would be voting on a severance package and a recommendation to dissolve the pastoral relationship between me and the church, I knew it was going to be difficult, possibly contentious; upsetting to a lot of folks; painful in ways that mere words cannot describe.

Little wonder that I had not been sleeping well this week. Little wonder that I was a tad bit cranky (to put it mildly). Little wonder that I woke up this morning with a sour stomach which only became more disagreeable as the morning went on. Even a simple breakfast of toast and tea didn't produce the hoped for results.

So, as I got ready to head over to the church, I grabbed a bottle of generic pink medicine just in case the stomach didn't become a better patient and tossed it into my cloth bag with the rest of my Sunday go-to-meetin' stuff. As I said goodbye to Bonnie, who was leaving on the morning walk with Dusty the Church Dog, she said, "Too bad you can't have Dusty sitting beside you during church this morning. That would make it a lot better." I mumbled an agreement and went out the door.

When I got to the church, I did my usual Sunday routine of unlocking all the entrances, opening up the Sunday School rooms, turning on the lights, checking the phone machine, yada, yada yada.

Then, I went back to my office to try to muck together some words that, if I was lucky (and I don't think I was), would resemble a sermon.

About half way through this process, my stomach decided to release another dose of acid, so I reached into the cloth bag, hoping to find my trusty little bottle of relief.

But what I found was something else. There, in the bottom of the bag, amidst the pens, papers, books, and other pastoral detritus was a cloth giraffe, one of Dusty's favorite toys. He wasn't allowed to come to church (after all, dogs have neither voice nor vote in our system), so he sent a representative to be with me.

Now, I know that giraffe was not in that bag when I put stuff in it last night before going to bed and trying to sleep. Bonnie swears that she did not do it. And the cat would never stoop so low as to touch one of the dog's toys.

But there it was, right where I would find it when I needed some relief, some help, some hope, some assurance.

And Dusty? When confronted with the evidence, he just cocked his head, looked at me with those big brown eyes, and smiled . . .

I think just about every person who has come into my office the last week or so has said the same thing, "I'm having trouble with forgiving." And, I can relate to that. Because there is a lot of forgiving that I am having trouble doing.

What bothers me, though, are the folks who say, "I will never forgive . . ." or "I cannot receive communion from so-and-so . . ." or "if they nominate her/him/them to serve on the Session, I will . . "

So, I am starting to realize that in God's good wisdom, we are going to be saying goodbye during Eastertide. That season when, it seems to me, just about every gospel story stares us in the face and says, 'what are you going to do with the risen Christ?' I find it fascinating that in these stories, Jesus just shows up, uninvited, unknown, unexpected.

He doesn't knock on the door of the room where the disciples are hiding - he knows they will all hold their breath, hoping that whoever is knocking will think no one is home, and just go away. No, he just pops up in their midst.

He doesn't flag us down for a ride. He just appears in the back seat of the car as we are driving home from church, and startles us by asking 'what are you folks talking about?'

He doesn't come looking for a job on our fishing boat, or in our church, or at the school, or in the workplace. He just pushes his food trolley along the way, asking if we are hungry.

Because he wants to feed us, he wants to nourish us, he wants to fill us - with peace, with hope, with forgiveness, with grace, with healing. And not just us, but all those folks we cannot abide (and maybe who feel the same way about us); all those folks whose hands we don't want to shake or hold (and who may not want our touch, either); all those people we just can't believe God has put us together with in this place called the church.

And he just stands there, with that little ironic smile that has been on God's face from the first moment of creation, asking, 'now, what are you going to do?'

I recently read an article which talked about how many of the old Scottish Highland croft houses contained two rooms. The outer room was known as the 'but' and this was the place where formal visits were made. You know - when the doctor, the insurance person, the minister knocked on the door, this is where you sat and talked with these folks.

There was also an inner room, known as the 'ben.' This was where the family gathered, this was the room of warmth, of laughter, of tears, of celebration, of people being able to be themselves, and not having to put on a 'company face' and formal manners. The highest compliment a guest could be paid was, when you knocked on the door, to be greeted with a smile, a door opened wide, and given the wonderfully inviting greeting, "Come awa' ben."

I wonder how many of the folks who come to church for the first (or second, or beyond) time feel like they are received into the outer room of the church. They are welcomed, yes, but formally, officially, even (sad to say) begrudgingly. They are talked to, formally, officially, even begrudgingly. They are given a cup of coffee or tea, but it seems it is served in the company china, accompanied by the company manners, the company faces. Yet, what they are simply longing for is to be invited into the place where the family gathers, with laughter and joy and shared lives, handed a steaming cup in an old and chipped mug, being treated as a long lost sister or brother.

And I wonder how often, when I have invited God into my life, it is officially, formally, begrudgingly; with my company manners, my company face, my company formality, when all God is longing for is to hear those hospitable words "come awa' ben."

I sat down on the front pew to listen to the postlude by our guest musician, a concert pianist. I was close enough to observe the delicacy of his fingers on the softer notes, and the arching hands that gave force to the stronger. The piece echoed in the sanctuary as he played, no music in front of him, simply from memory.

How is it that one person hears notes in their head (where I only hear noise) and puts them down on sheets of paper, shaping them into a piece that endures through the centuries? How does one memorize the complexity of the notes, and then send them down to her fingertips, playing them in such a way that still echoes in hearts hours and days later? I could pick out the notes on a piano, but could never put them together so that people's lives are changed.

How is it that I can look at a field and see trees, grass, a couple of horses, a sky with clouds gathering darkly, and a Constable sees 'The Hay Wain'? How is it that I can put words together in a rambling sentence, and a poet can take those same words and produce something that calls you to sit in silence?

How is it that I can look at a scene and quickly dismiss it as every day ordinary, and a photographer snaps a picture and through her eyes that same image resonates with thousands of people? How is it that I can see an injustice and write a letter to the editor, and a Lincoln can pen his 'House Divided' speech?

More and more, it is in the notes in the musician's head and hands, it is the internal eyes of the painter and photographer, it is in the dexterity of the wordsmith that I find confirmation that we are indeed created in the image of God, the Master Artisan.

scraps

I have started the arduous task of cleaning out my office. Which is proving to be more of an undertaking than I originally thought. I am now seriously considering throwing everything out and simply starting over again!

But as I was weeding through all those marvelous file folders marked with titles that seemed so important years ago when I wrote them down, and put the article torn from the newspaper/magazine (and which I have not pulled out once since sticking it in the file cabinet), I came across my old friend, "Scraps."

This is the folder where I throw in thoughts, snippets, words and images that dart across my mind at all sorts of inappropriate moments (like sleeping), but strike me as fodder for some liturgy, poem, prayer in the future. There are quotes that I jot down on napkins, or backs of bulletins, or whatever is handy, that I figure might be good for some sermon in the future.

So, I started playing with those scraps of paper, these good and comfortable old friends, and rediscovered a quote that I have no idea where it came from originally, but I obviously liked when I first read it: "Take your heart and throw it over the fence. Then jump over it." Isn't that marvelous?

Isn't that what all the post-Resurrection stories are about? The willingness to look beyond the fishing boat, the road we are traveling, the doubts and wonders that get in our way, and to leap over that fence and discover the garden that God has been planting for us.

Isn't that what I need to do in the coming days, weeks, and months? I have no clear vision of where God is leading me/us next. I have not tripped over any burning bush and scorched myself. I haven't had any dreams from God telling me to go to Egypt, or New York, or wherever. But this quote reminds me that out there, over that fence, just over the horizon, just over the hurdles of my fears and worries, lies whatever future God has in place for me.

Isn't that what we are all called to do in following Jesus? He's already climbed over that fence called death, and is ahead of us.

Let's throw our hearts over and go jumping after him.

God bless you, Dusty!

Dusty the Church Dog never met a bad day. If it was snowing, that meant going down to the nearby school and racing around the fields; it meant making doggy snow angels in the front yard, and catching snowballs no matter how hard they were thrown. If it was raining, it meant splashing through puddles, and rolling in the front yard until he was soaked to the skin. If it was a crisp fall day, it meant walking down around the lake (or perhaps the campground with the great smells) looking for the Biscuit Lady, who always had treats for him. If it was a clear spring day, there was nothing better than sitting on the lawn, smelling the leaves uncurling, the dandelions poking their heads up out of the earth, the birds building their nests in the trees.

Dusty the Church Dog never met a person he didn't immediately like and turn into his new BFF. From the curmudgeonly neighbor who always had a frown on his face and a complaint on his lips to the little kid trying out his bicycle with training wheels, Dusty just had to meet them, had to greet them, had to turn their day into the tail-waggingest one they had ever had. He enjoyed meeting other dogs, especially the little guys in the neighborhood, and managed to give a wide berth to any cats he met. Squirrels always found a tree to run up, rabbits always seemed to bounce further when they saw him, and deer utterly confused him.

Dusty the Church Dog touched lives in ways in which I can only dream of doing. He would turn those big brown eyes towards the face of the woman sitting in the hallway at the nursing home, and her face would beam with delight.

He read books by the dozens to kids on Thursday mornings and taught them how much fun it was to catch a carrot in midair and crunch it to pieces.

He showed incredible patience in waiting for his turn at the ice cream place (but don't try to jump the line in front of him!), and he gave unconcitional love and acceptance to everyone he met, even if simply passing on the street.

Dusty the Church Dog was my confidant, my trusted companion, my faithful sidekick, my window into the grace, the love, the wonder, the power, the joy of God which is always around us. He was the one who got me out of bed to listen to the geese flying south. He was the one who taught me that there is always something to experience, someone to meet, some marvelous delight just waiting around the next corner. He was the one who couldn't wait to experience the next moment which was coming into his life. He was the one who got me through some of the toughest days of ministry, of our struggles with Teddy, of life itself.

Sadly, Dusty the Church Dog finally met something that didn't love him, that wouldn't give in to his silly smile and gentle nature, that wouldn't let him keep going through this life. A tumor on his spleen that was causing internal bleeding meant that those who loved him so much and would miss him beyond any possible words could describe, had to help him cross that Rainbow Bridge into peace, gentleness, and everlasting joy. So, about an hour ago, we held him, hugged him, whispered our thanks to him as he closed his eyes one last time this side of life.

And you will never, ever convince me that the wet streets and sidewalks we discovered when we came out of the vet's office were simply from a passing shower.

Thom M. Shuman is a graduate of Eckerd College (St. Petersburg, FL) and Union Presbyterian Seminary (Richmond, VA). Currently active in transitional/interim ministry, he has served churches in Oklahoma, Virginia, and Ohio. His liturgies, poems, and prayers are used by congregations all over the world, and by individuals for personal devotions.

His Advent devotional books *The Jesse Tree* (2005) and *Gobsmacked* (2011) have been published by Wild Goose Publications/The Iona Community (www.icnabooks.com), as well as his wedding liturgy, *Now Come Two Hearts,* and *Lenten and Easter Nudges* (PDF download). He is also a contributor to the Iona Community's Resource books *Candles & Conifers, Hay & Stardust, Fire and Bread, Bare Feet and Buttercups,* and *Acorns and Archangels,* as well as *Going Home Another Way: Daily Readings and Resources for Christmastide, Gathered and Scattered: Readings and Meditations from the Iona Community, 50 New Prayers From The Iona Community,* and *Like Leaves to the Sun, Prayers from the Iona Community.*

Playing Hopscotch in Heaven. Lectionary Liturgies for RCL Year A, as well as a companion book, *Piano Man, poems and prayers for RCL Year A* have just been published.

Bearers of Grace and Justice. Lectionary Liturgies for Year C as well as a companion book, *Pirate Jesus, Poems and Prayers for RCL Lectionary Year C* were published in 2012.

He blogs at www.occasionalsightings.blogspot.com
www.prayersfortoday.blogspot.com
www.lectionaryliturgies.blogspot.com

Cover photo: Thom M. Shuman

Printed in Great Britain
by Amazon

37123201R00050